AF470067

CAMERA ABOVE THE CLOUDS
Volume 2

CAMERA ABOVE THE CLOUDS

Volume 2

The Aviation Photographs of Charles E. Brown

Edited by Anthony Harold

Airlife
England

ISBN 0 906393 50 7

First published 1985
by Airlife Publishing Ltd.

Airlife Publishing Ltd.

7 St. John's Hill, Shrewsbury, England.

Printed in England by Livesey Ltd., Shrewsbury.

Foreword

by Harald Penrose

In the course of five decades Charles Brown was a familiar figure regarded with affection by every test pilot (and many another) of the British aircraft industry. He was so modest, so trustworthy, yet firm in explaining exactly how he wanted us to fly our prototypes in relation to his allotted photographic machine and the angle of sunlight, for even before take-off he had in his mind's eye a sequence of compositions.

Whenever feasible he preferred these sorties to be above cloudscape, and even with close-ups at lower heights we would fly on and on until there was an appropriate laterally distant cloud formation or outstanding countryside or coastal configuration. In those earliest days until well into World War II there was no radio available for instant communication, so we relied on hand signals. Our pre-flight briefing was therefore thorough, and once airborne the mission usually took an hour for Charles to take his carefully selected shots which invariably were rewarding masterpieces when acknowledgement copies were received a few days later.

Finding a suitable aeroplane in which to ensconce him was often a difficulty unless of the same type as his subject such as Lysander to Lysander, which at least had similar performance; but when we could only provide a light aeroplane with restrictive cockpit from which to photograph a swiftly passing fighter, he never complained and his results were just as brilliant as when photographing from a larger cabin aircraft with window or door temporarily removed to ensure direct vision for his camera.

His occupation has its risk of collision when manoeuvring close passes and steeply banked turns, but the only time I ever found him discomforted was when invited to fly as passenger in a balloon piloted by a famous French aeronaut at the first of the Royal Aeronautical Society's Garden Parties held after the Second World War. 'I didn't like it a bit', he said. 'In that barely waist-high, swaying basket it was just like standing giddily on the edge of a precipice, so I didn't take a thing except the crowd'.

But perhaps that apprehension was the consequence of the alarming sight, when a lad, of a balloon crashing onto a suburban roof and tipping out its crew. He photographed the dramatic scene and initiated his long career, for he sold the print to the *Daily Mirror*; as a result he was given a job in their photographic department — though in my day he was a famous freelance, and we even felt honoured that this very likeable man should visit our factory from time to time, for his splendid photographs were wonderful publicity'!

More importantly, the full range of his aeronautical subjects, whether of specific aircraft or great occasions such as RAF Displays, is of great historical interest, and Charles must have been very gratified that his unique collection is safe for posterity in the care of the Royal Air Force Museum.

Introduction

Some of the richest photographic images of aeroplanes in flight have been the result of one man's activity. That man was Charles E. Brown who was without doubt a great press photographer, a greater part of whose working life was devoted to the discipline of aviation photography.

He learnt the skills of a photographer at the age of fourteen when he joined the staff of the *Daily Mirror*, working first as a processor and progressing quickly to become an assignment photographer when he was given varied briefs throughout the first world war. His first successful picture was the 'Balloon on the roof' which he took in 1911 with his first camera. The newsworthy aspect of this work probably led to the use of this photograph by the *Daily Mirror*, but through his initiative a firm offer of employment was made to the young man and accepted.

It was not until the late twenties that his specialisation in aviation photography began and there is very little evidence to suggest that Charles Brown was especially interested in aviation in the past, even though he spent a brief period at the end of the Great War in the RAF.

Photographing railways proved more compelling in the mechanical subject sphere until, through the excellence of his work, he was able to get commissions from Captain Clarke of the Admiralty press division and from Charles Robertson of the Air Ministry Public Relations Department.

Now he had the opportunity to photograph aircraft of the Royal Air Force both at sea and over land and his business, which he began in 1921, never looked back.

Charles Brown poses before a photographic session with Fairey's historic aircraft. White Waltham 1956.

Charles Brown in his later years seated in a Middle East Airlines Comet.

The facilities he was offered were considerable but were enhanced by the goodwill Charles Brown himself engendered and anyone on an assignment who was involved received photographs of the highest quality. The guaranteed quality of his photographs and the quick and thorough distribution of his work certainly ensured that he would always be offered official assignments.

To support his output it was necessary for him to run a processing and printing facility and to keep working records of the work he carried out. A large collection of prints linked with negatives were kept for immediate reference and a surplus of prints were also produced to allow for instant service.

It is from this collection of black and white prints that the images presented in these two 'Camera above the Clouds' volumes, have been selected.

The final values and definition and composition are, where possible, those which C. E. Brown himself passed for publication. They represent, in many cases, the whole negative area and give a much greater feeling of space and contrast than the cropped images finally used in so many publications in the past.

The purpose of both the first and second volumes of 'Camera above the Clouds' is to bring together some of the finest photographs taken by C. E. Brown during his remarkable career. It is not an encyclopaedia of aircraft or a complete illustrated catalogue of his aviation photographs. If several photographs are reproduced representing the same aircraft it is because each photograph has some intrinsic quality of light or space or composition which makes it an outstanding aviation photograph.

The collection of Charles E. Brown photographs is treasured by the Royal Air Force Museum who have owned and administered it since his death in 1978, aged 86.

It has been extremely difficult to elucidate much about the modest man behind the camera besides the bare details of his addresses and dates of change, but in his working life-time he did write a couple of articles to support his published photographs and these we have reproduced in full on the following pages so that his own words will be linked with this volume of photographs.

Pictures in the air Charles E. Brown

"Get that?"

"What a hope." I had scarcely even seen it.

My pilot's question came as we flashed past, in opposite direction, the aeroplane we were trying to photograph. It is impossible for me to say whether it passed above or below us as I do not know which way up we were. "We had better land and talk to him". A definitely tricky job this, we had to take the other fellow flying upside down.

The photography of aircraft in straight flight is simple 'IF'. The big "if" is that conference on the ground before the two planes, known as the photographic machine and the target machine, take off. It must be settled beforehand which side the target plane is to fly, the height and the course. The position of the sun usually controls the last factor according to the direction of lighting required in the picture. Signals are also pre-arranged as it is impossible to convey any variation of plans from one machine to the other during flight except by pointing or waving of the arms but the photographer has communication with his own pilot by means of voice pipes.

Nothing must be left to chance, it is useless taking off with the idea that all will work out right in the air. It will not. And besides, minutes are valuable. I have been up to photograph an aircraft which was consuming petrol at the rate of nearly three gallons a minute, the total running costs in such a case are terrific, the photographic machine must also be powerful with consequent high cost of flying if it is to keep up speed with its objective.

We now take off, climb to the appointed height, our aerial "sitter" approaches from behind and "formates" on us, the pilot watching meanwhile for the photographer to indicate final instructions as to his exact position, the camera shutter clicks and all is finished. In five minutes we are on the aerodrome again expressing satisfaction at the job having been completed so quickly. It is not always so easy as this. Perhaps we have to take a fast new type of aircraft whose minimum speed is greater than our own maximum, in this case formation flying is impossible and the picture must be taken while it is flying past. While this does not necessarily involve any difficulty it does hinder the exact choice of angle. Early last year I flew for two hundred miles trying to catch up to a big flying boat which it had been arranged should fly alongside and we were unable to understand why it did not wait for us but flew on its course at a speed entirely beyond our range.

On arrival at our destination we learned from the pilot that as soon as he got in the air he was informed by wireless that a storm was imminent and he was to reach his destination without delay — an advantage of being equipped with wireless that we did not share. Although we dodged the worst of the gale the pilot was almost the only occupant of the big boat to escape a violent attack of airsickness. On another occasion I went up from Croydon to take a series of air liners in flight. My own machine was by no means a slow one but we were only able to catch one out of four, sad to relate that was the British one.

To revert to the incident with which this article opened, the task was the much more difficult one of photographing a man "flying on his back". Inverted flying is a whole time job for the pilot and one cannot expect much co-operation from him in other matters, so the photographic machine has to do all the positioning. In order to be alongside at the vital moment, careful calculations must be made allowing for loss of height and speed in getting into the inverted position and even then steep banking turns and dives almost amounting to aerobatics may be necessary to bring us alongside in time before he has to roll over again to normal. While some types of aircraft can fly upside down for only a few seconds others can go on indefinitely without losing height. Sometimes the further complication arises of a particular landmark being required as a background. It is true that this may occasionally be printed in afterwards but the result is never so satisfactory and the real art of the aerial photographer lies in producing the picture at the time. Subsequent faking is but a disguise for a job improperly done.

Aerial photography is now employed for a great many purposes. Manufacturing companies want pictures of their factories; records of progress of construction of buildings and estates are regularly taken; holiday resorts can in an air view show their layout and their amenities at a glance and in this way they are used considerably for propaganda purposes. An aerial view of a vessel passing through the water will demonstrate to the designer, by the waves set up, the effect of his streamlining. Newspapers now show the great events which are all going on in the making of the world's history in the same way. All these come into the class of subjects known as "Obliques", i.e. where the camera is held at an oblique angle in relation to the ground below.

Then come the "Verticals" which comprise a highly specialised branch of the work. For these the camera, instead of being held over the side of the plane, is fixed in the bottom of the fuselage and points directly downwards. The results are not pictorial and are often unintelligible to the non-technical observer as nearly all sense of relief is destroyed. Thousands of miles of country have been surveyed in this way by the joining up of consecutively taken photographs. Special cameras are employed for this purpose and truly wonderful instruments they are! Controlled by electricity, they can be set to go on taking on a long roll of film without further attention. Exposures are made at regular intervals and each bears the impression of a watch and a compass and so shows both time and bearing. It is important that the pilot flies at a constant height and on an exactly even keel. Similar methods are employed in the photography of enemy trenches and emplacements in time of war. During the last war, before these special cameras were available, there was keen competition between squadrons of the Royal Air Force to produce the largest "mosaic" of the enemy's territory. Some of these ran into many hundreds of separate photographs pasted together.

The sun is always shining although we do not always enjoy the benefits of it on the ground. Frequently when the taking of aerial views is impossible we may continue with the photography of aircraft in flight by the simple process of going up through the clouds into the sunshine above. There is no more thrilling sight than the dazzling whiteness surmounted by blue sky which greets us after penetrating the cold, damp layer which is shrouding the city below and there is no more beautiful background for our pictures.

Except for the survey work to which I have already referred, little modification is required to the ordinary camera for aerial purposes. The principal difference is that a box replaces bellows which do not withstand the severe wind pressure. A high speed shutter, preferably of the focal plane type, is essential and a light filter of yellow or pale green is incorporated in the lens in order to help penetrate the haze which exists in varying degrees in the English atmosphere. Naturally one uses the fastest plates or films available, personally I favour plates. It is customary to advise the pilot when a photograph is being taken, he then throttles back the engine to reduce speed and vibration.

I am happy to say that my experience does not include the usual thrills and hairsbreadth escapes of which one so often reads from those who pursue their vocation in the air, this may be due in part to a temperament which places complete confidence in the pilot and relying on him to extricate us from what another might interpret as a tight corner. I am convinced that danger is often imagined where none exists, particularly by persons travelling as passengers with nothing else to occupy their attentions. I have been far more frightened when landing in a fog in an airliner than by anything which has happened when I have been in the air working. Flying at great height over Alps or skimming low over housetops or sea only become disturbing at the moment one commences to doubt the pilot's mastery over the situation. I would not suggest that things invariably go exactly according to plan, maybe the pilot himself is experiencing more cause for anxiety at moments when I am too engrossed with my work to feel concerned; this has repeatedly been confessed to me afterwards. Such a case occurred when through an error of judgement in landing on the deck of an aircraft carrier we nearly landed in the sea instead. Again, I remember once having to photograph a mimic aerial combat in which a plane was supposed to be shot out of control, catch fire in the air and fall to the ground in flames. As a prelude to this the pilot released smoke from a cylinder and looped the loop; we had all overlooked the fact that in so doing he would be looping back into his own smoke and obscuring his view. It was the quick appreciation of the situation and skill of my pilot that averted a collision. The pilot is responsible for the safety of his passenger, his aircraft and himself. The thought that he has his own reasons for desiring to remain alive should always be comforting to those taking the air as passengers, particularly for the first time. The photographer, on the other hand, is apt to be unmindful of danger and the technicalities of aviation in his desire to produce the best possible picture.

When fulfilling a commission to take a close view of a small ship under sail the following conversation took place. I had for some time been persuading the pilot to fly nearer and nearer the water —

Pilot: Brown, you realise this is a land machine?

Self: Yes.

Pilot: But suppose the engine cuts!

Self: It never has done before.

Pilot: But you mustn't count on that.

Self: Chance it.

A Pause

Pilot: Can you swim?
Self: Fairly well. Can you?
Pilot: Not too well.

After the photos were taken —

Self: O.K., we can go back now.
Pilot: Brown, you would be a more likeable fellow if you weren't so ------- enthusiastic.

Thank goodness pilots do not do all they are asked. Photographers do need some restraining.

The World below from the World above

Charles E. Brown

"Go up and take a photograph of —". To many men, to whom a few years ago this order would have brought a thrill, the feeling of being assigned a task of out-of-the-ordinary importance, it is now a routine instruction.

In civil life aerial photography may be divided broadly into two categories, Press and Commercial. The commercial purposes are concerned largely with advertising; the manufacturer requiring views of his works; the hotelier who wants to show in his latest booklet how his hotel is surrounded by gardens, its proximity to the seashore or how just a short road leads guests to the golf course. The engineer often keeps a photographic record of progress of construction and the borough surveyor a record of the growth of the town's new housing scheme. The photographer of such subjects usually has the advantage of choosing his day — when the weather is favourable.

Weather is the paramount factor in the work. Since the war great strides have been made in the manufacture of photographic plates and films; they are faster and sensitive to a longer range colours, lenses also are faster. Filters may be used to eliminate some of the mist but not all of it. Despite all these modern aids perfection can only be achieved when the atmosphere is clear and the sun shining.

The flying Pressman has not the advantage of choosing his weather. When news "breaks" he flies — and makes the most of it. There is a fire at the sawmills near the docks, a liner aground off the coast of Cornwall or a big railway smash. He is speeding by car to the nearest aerodrome while the pilot is warming up the engine of the aircraft. There have been cases where the risks run in the gathering of news photographs have been too great to be justified and disaster has resulted, but we are not at the moment concerned with the ethics of the job. Do it and argue afterwards is the rule. But it is not only disasters in which the aerial view is useful, it often provides the best impression of historic ceremonies; the launching of a big ship for example. The unveiling of many of the war memorials in France and Belgium were illustrated in this way. The use for this purpose is however limited in the case of ceremonies taking place in towns or cities owing to the restrictions of low flying.

Aerial photography is team work. The closest possible co-operation between the photographer and his pilot is essential. It is an advantage if the two can constantly work together, each getting to know the other's methods. If the object to be taken is stationary we shall probably fly several circles round it, selecting the angles and height from which to work. Finally, as each shot is approached, we fly a little higher than the level from which the photograph will be taken. The pilot is warned, he throttles back the engine to minimise forward speed and vibration and in doing so sinks to the required altitude. Having got into this position it may be necessary to turn the machine slightly to port or starboard in order to clear wing tips from the line of vision. When photographing objects moving on the surface, such as ships at sea, the procedure is much the same except that allowance has to be made for the changing position of the objective.

To me, the most exciting branch of aerial photography is that of taking aircraft in flight. Flying alongside a new aeroplane during trials is always fascinating, seeing its characteristic points, spotting its angles and comparing its speed with ones own and other aircraft. Here, as in no other branch of the work is one free from weather conditions except for gales or dense fog.

Air pictures are no longer a novelty, they no longer justify themselves simply because they are taken in the sky any more than a snapshot somewhere on Epsom Downs would faithfully illustrate the race for the Derby. Composition must be studied and backgrounds, they must be pictorially right. If it be a land machine a suitable land background would be chosen. Supposing it had been given the type name of Salisbury one would endeavour to include the cathedral with its famous spire. If a seaplane or flying boat, coastal scenery would be selected or even open sea.

It is, however, not infrequently the case that visibility is poor and the surface screened by dark grey clouds. It is then that we use the silver lining for our background, a visit to the blue sky above is an ever welcome excursion and I know many airmen with countless flying hours to their credit who still get a thrill from the celestial panorama of blue and dazzling white with its clean, crisp air which greets them on emerging from the moisture saturated shroud which keeps the sun's rays from the city below. Those silly little people down in London! Why don't they come up and enjoy the fresh air? An enormous sense of superiority claims one up here. You know that feeling out tramping at crack of dawn on a Spring morning when all else are sleeping? It is that amplified. You are on top of the world. And what material there is up there, huge billowing masses, dips and hollows, here and there a hole where mother earth is just visible. There are forms and shapes innumerable against which to place the target which may be a single 'plane, a flight or a squadron also there is a vast range of lighting effects. We may be taking "down sun" with all its vivid brightness or taking silhouettes on the shadow side against varying shades of grey.

The accessibility of these regions varies greatly with the machines in use at the time. Quite recently the officer commanding a squadron of Royal Air Force fighters remarked on finding conditions bad near the ground "We will pop up and take the photographs above the clouds, we ought to find nice weather at twelve thousand". And we did. A few minutes flying that's all. To a small civil machine with lower rate of climb this would be a task of some magnitude. I remember going up from Croydon to take a new small passenger airliner and was being flown myself in an old aircraft. It took so long to gain the necessary height that by the time the photographs were taken we were over the coast.

The actual photography is very little different from that on the ground and can be done with standard apparatus so long as the camera has a sufficiently high shutter speed. My own is an ordinary hand camera bought before the war but has recently been modified by conversion into a box camera by replacing the bellows with wood. This became increasingly necessary as the speed of aircraft increased, when the camera with leather bellows is held over the side of the fuselage the slip-stream is almost sure to blow them in.

The communication between pilot and photographer in the air is mostly done through the voice pipe but last minute instructions are often more conveniently conveyed by hand signals as they usually prove quicker. For this reason big flying boats are ideal as there is generally a seat in front of the pilot and the passing of signs is rendered extremely simple. There are, of course other factors which make some aircraft much better photographic machines than others. I prefer the type in which one remains standing in the cockpit rather than seated. This applies particularly in Service machines where the safety regulations are indeed rigid. As a case in point, I flew in a light bomber during last year's Air Defence of Great Britain exercises. As we had to go to a great height an oxygen mask had to be worn in addition to heavy overalls, we were going over the sea so a pneumatic flotation waistcoat was insisted upon and then the regulation parachute. It will be seen that with all these encumbrances one's movement is so restricted that from a sitting position it would be extremely difficult to manipulate the camera successfully. When we were very high up I inadvertently disconnected my telephone and my pilot was unable to tell me to start using oxygen — an instruction I was waiting for and thinking I was going to "pass out" meanwhile, but this is by the way. Sometimes it is the pilot who is having the trying time, particularly when flying low. The photographer in his anxiety to get a close shot is oblivious of dangers of which the pilot, eager to help, is vividly conscious.

There are other purposes for which photography is employed in the Royal Air Force. The bursts during bombing practise give an exact record of the accuracy or otherwise of the aiming. In the Fleet Air Arm the fall of shot from ships is similarly recorded. Then there is the ingenious "camera gun", looking very much like a machine gun, used for aerial target practise. The gunner fires bullets at another aeroplane so each pressing of the trigger takes a photograph and the film when developed records the number of "hits"

Lastly there is "vertical" photography — where the camera is pointing exactly vertically at the ground; it is used for survey work and, in time of war for taking enemy territory to study his lines of trenches, gun emplacements etc. These photographs are so highly technical that they are often unintelligible to the lay observer. They are certainly uninteresting pictorially as the sense of contour is destroyed.

VICKERS VIRGINIA X

Vickers Virginia X drops packages by parachute as a demonstration of airborne supply capability at one of the Royal Air Force Displays at Hendon. Some 160 Virginia bombers were built for the Royal Air Force and once the type had been superseded as the Service's heavy bomber, it still remained in use until 1937, thirteen years after it first began squadron use.

SHORT SINGAPORE III

In September 1935, Singapore III's of No. 203 Squadron flew submarine co-operation patrols and transported mail during the Ethiopian invasion by Mussolini. In 1936 the Squadron was based at Basra, where these aeroplanes where photographed; No. 203 Squadron would continue to fly Short Singapores until February 1940.

HAWKER DEMONS *(opposite)*

Hawker Demons of No. 23 Squadron. The Hawker Demon was a variant of the highly successful Hart Bomber and brought back the First World War concept of a two-seat fighter. Its speed in 1933 exceeded that of the RAF's standard fighter, the Bristol Bulldog, which it replaced in No. 23 Squadron. When production ceased in 1937, a total of 234 Demons had been built for the RAF. With a Rolls-Royce Kestrel 115 engine, the Demon was capable of a maximum speed of 182 mph at 16,400 feet.

K2844
K
3782
K3782
K
3784
K3784
K
2853
K2853

WESTLAND WALLACE

Westland Wallace, K3570 of No. 501 (City of Bristol) Squadron at the firing ranges in the Bristol Channel in 1933. The Wallace Mk I was a modified Wapiti and twelve aircraft were constructed which were issued to No. 501 Squadron of the Royal Auxiliary Air Force. In all some 172 Wallace Is and IIs were constructed and the type, described as a two-seat general purpose aircraft, equipped four squadrons of the Royal Auxiliary Air Force. Many found a use as target towing aircraft when superseded. The last were retired in 1943.

SHORT SINGAPORE III
The Singapore was to become an important flying boat in RAF Service both at home and overseas. The first MkIIIs were available in June 1934 and production finally ceased in 1937 when a total of 37 had been constructed.
The Singapore III was powered by four Rolls-Royce Kestrel engines which gave the aircraft a range of 1,000 miles at a cruising speed of 105 mph.

FAIREY HENDON II, K5085.
The Fairey Hendon II became the RAF's first all metal low wing cantilever monoplane heavy bomber and although the prototype first flew in 1931, it was not until 1937 that the first and only batch of 14 aircraft were delivered to No. 38 Squadron at Marham. Powered by the Rolls-Royce Kestrel VI engines the Hendon could carry 1,600 lbs of bombs, 1300 miles at 133 mph. In 1932 it was a great step forward but by the time it was ordered into production it was already superseded by the next generation of heavy bombers and quantity contracts were dropped.

HANDLEY PAGE HEYFORD
The Handley Page Heyford became the RAF's last biplane heavy night bomber, entering service with No. 99 Squadron at Upper Heyford in November 1933. Powered by two Rolls-Royce Kestrel engines the Heyford could fly a 1,600lb bomb load 900 miles at a maximum of 142 mph. In its Service life the type equipped eleven bomber Squadrons and when the Heyford began to be replaced in 1937, 124 had been produced. This photograph shows the distinctive layout of the Heyford, a shape that would still grace the skies in a variety of training duties until 1941.

BOULTON PAUL OVERSTRAND

Twenty-four Overstrand bombers were built for the RAF and they entered service in 1934 with No. 101 Squadron. Developed from its predecessor the Sidestrand, the Overstrand had more powerful engines which enhanced the types handling qualities, increased its bomb load and enabled it to be fitted with a power-operated enclosed gun turret.

Overstrands were superseded as first line bombers in 1937. K4561 was one of the last built and was probably photographed in 1936, prior to its appearance at the RAF Display at Hendon.

PERCIVAL MEW GULL
The prototype Mew Gull flew in March 1934 in the hands of its designer Edgar W. Percival. Re-engined with a 200 hp Gipsy Six the tiny aeroplane was capable of 191 mph.

HAWKER HINDS
Hawker Hinds of No. 139 Squadron flying in formation over Hendon airfield. The fabulous array of aircraft on the ground are assembled for the annual RAF display.

TRANS-ATLANTIC TRIALS
The first refuelled trans-Atlantic service commenced on 5th August 1939. The modified Short S30 flying boat *Cabot* was refuelled, after take off, with 5,000 lbs of fuel from a Harrow tanker before leaving the Southampton area. To complete its crossing *Cabot* would refuell again over Newfoundland, the service lasted briefly due to the outbreak of war.

FAIREY BATTLE
The Battle was one of the main aircraft types supplied to the RAF during the Expansion Scheme period and between 1937 and 1939 it was to equip an entire Group of Bomber Command. This photograph is of K7578, a Fairey Battle of No. 105 Squadron based at Harwell in November 1937.

SHORT MERCURY SEAPLANE

Short Mercury seaplane taxies in the Medway. This little aeroplane was part of a very remarkable experiment inspired by Major R. H. Mayo who reasoned that a large flying boat could carry a smaller aircraft part way to a destination, thereafter the smaller machine could be detached and fly with full tanks and a normally excessive load, very great distances, Pairing a specially designed variant of the S.23 Empire flying boat called *Maia* and the Mercury, Shorts succeeded and in July 1938 a trans-Atlantic crossing was completed. The war brought further developments to a halt.

LOCKHEED 10A ELECTRA

Lockheed 10A Electra of British Airways could carry up to 10 passengers at a crusing speed of 185 mph. The Electras entered service in 1937 on the Croydon-Hamburg-Copenhagen-Malmo-Stockholm route. The Prime Minister Nevill Chamberlain flew in an Electra to meet Adolf Hitler at Munich in 1938 and subsequently used Charles E. Brown's photograph for his Christmas card.

GLOSTER GLADIATORS *(opposite)*

Although not the first squadron to receive Gladiators, No. 87 Squadron was to achieve acclaim for its expertise in the use of the aircraft for formation aerobatics. These three Gladiators are posing for the camera during the summer of 1938.

K
7968
K7968
K
7969
K
7972
K7972

GLOSTER GLADIATOR
A pleasing study of the last biplane fighter to enter RAF service. Powered by a Bristol Mercury IX engine, the Gladiator could achieve 233 mph at 14,500 feet and was highly manouevrable

SHORT 'EMPIRE' FLYING BOATS
Short Empire flying boats of Imperial Airways, introduced in 1936. No less than forty-five of these magnificent aeroplanes were produced; capable of carrying 24 day passengers or 16 night, they operated from the U.K. to Australia and South Africa. The early boats were S23s. Later aircraft fitted with more powerful engines were designated S30. This splendid photograph captures the panache of the Imperial Airways operation as a passenger launch, officials at attention, passes the moored S.23 *Cambria*.

AIRSPEED ENVOY
Painted royal blue and vermilion with silver trim, G-AEXX must have made a splendid sight as it posed for Charles Brown's camera. This Envoy was operated by the King's Flight, based at Hendon and was used by the Royal Household.
King George VI made a tour of RAF Stations during 1938, for which he used this aeroplane.

BOEING 314
A Boeing 314, making the first trans-Atlantic service appraisal for Pan Am, photographed in the Solent whilst Captain Grey and his crew prepare to leave their aircraft after its arrival. During the Second World War these aircraft would find much work flying the trans-Atlantic route to and from Northern Ireland and America.

AVRO ANSON I

Avro Anson I K6313 of No. 217 Squadron which became equipped with the type in March 1937 at Boscombe Down. Shortly after the squadron was to participate in the mass formation fly-past at the last Hendon Air Display. It was around this time that K6313 came to grief in a landing incident.

FALCON II GLIDER
Falcon II Glider dramatically photographed whilst being launched. The 'Bungee' method of launching, involving several strong volunteers and a large woven rubber band, was a standard method of glider launching at sites which had a hill suitable for soaring in the lift created by the prevailing wind. This picture was taken at Dunstable in 1939.

BRISTOL BLENHEIM I

The Bristol Blenheim entered service with the RAF in 1937 and made a considerable impact. It was considerably more advanced and much faster than the Hawker Hind light bombers it was designed to replace and it could outpace biplane fighters in service at the time.

During May 1937 No. 90 Squadron, based at Bicester, was equipped with Blenheim Is. This photograph of K7048 was taken by Charles Brown shortly after this, when the squadron was conducting Service development trials and giving flying demonstrations.

VICKERS WELLESLEY

Vickers Wellesley K8525 of No. 77 Squadron based at Honington in November 1937 when it first received the Wellesley. Designed by Vickers as a general purpose monoplane, the Wellesley was the first aeroplane to employ the geodetic construction. They were used by ten RAF Squadrons both at Home and overseas, and in the Middle East they carried out many successful bombing raids against the Axis powers. A part for which the Wellesley is most remembered is the 7,162 mile, non-stop flight carried out by three aircraft of the RAF Long-range Development Flight in 1938.

FAIREY SEA FOX

This Sea Fox K4305 was the second prototype which first flew in November 1936. The Sea Fox was designed as a light reconnaissance aeroplane which could be carried by and catapulted from Royal Navy cruisers. Some 64 aircraft were ordered following trials, the last production airframes being catapulted in April 1937.

In December 1939 the Sea Fox was to be used to great effect during the Battle of the River Plate when an aircraft from *Ajax* was employed to spot for the ship's guns.

The last Sea Fox unit disbanded in July 1943.

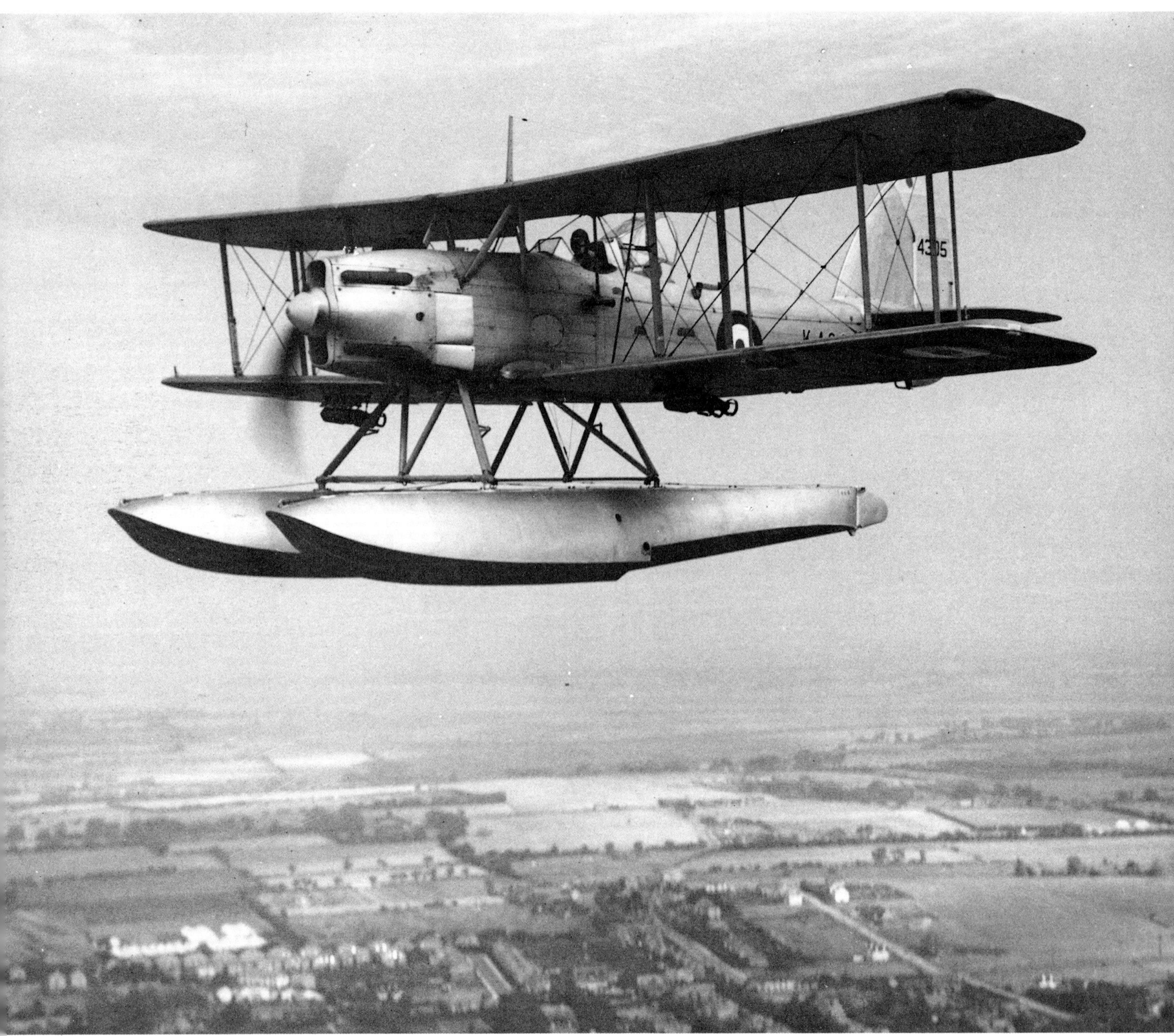

MILES MAGISTER I

Miles Magister I was the first monoplane training aircraft to be used by the RAF. Designed to provide a monoplane trainer in keeping with the expansion period fighters, the Magister was introduced in 1938 and was used by sixteen Elementary Flying Training Schools. Many passed into civil club use after the War when they became known as Hawk Trainer MkIIIs. L5933 was the twentieth of a total of 1,293 built and must have looked superb with its bright chrome yellow paint and polished cowlings.

CONCENTRATION
The pilot of an Airspeed Oxford I thinking about starting up! The Oxford entered service as a twin-engined monoplane, advanced trainer, in 1937.

MAINTENANCE
Fitters at work on a radial engine.

Native fire crew manning a Morris Commercial fire tender at Abu Suir in 1938.

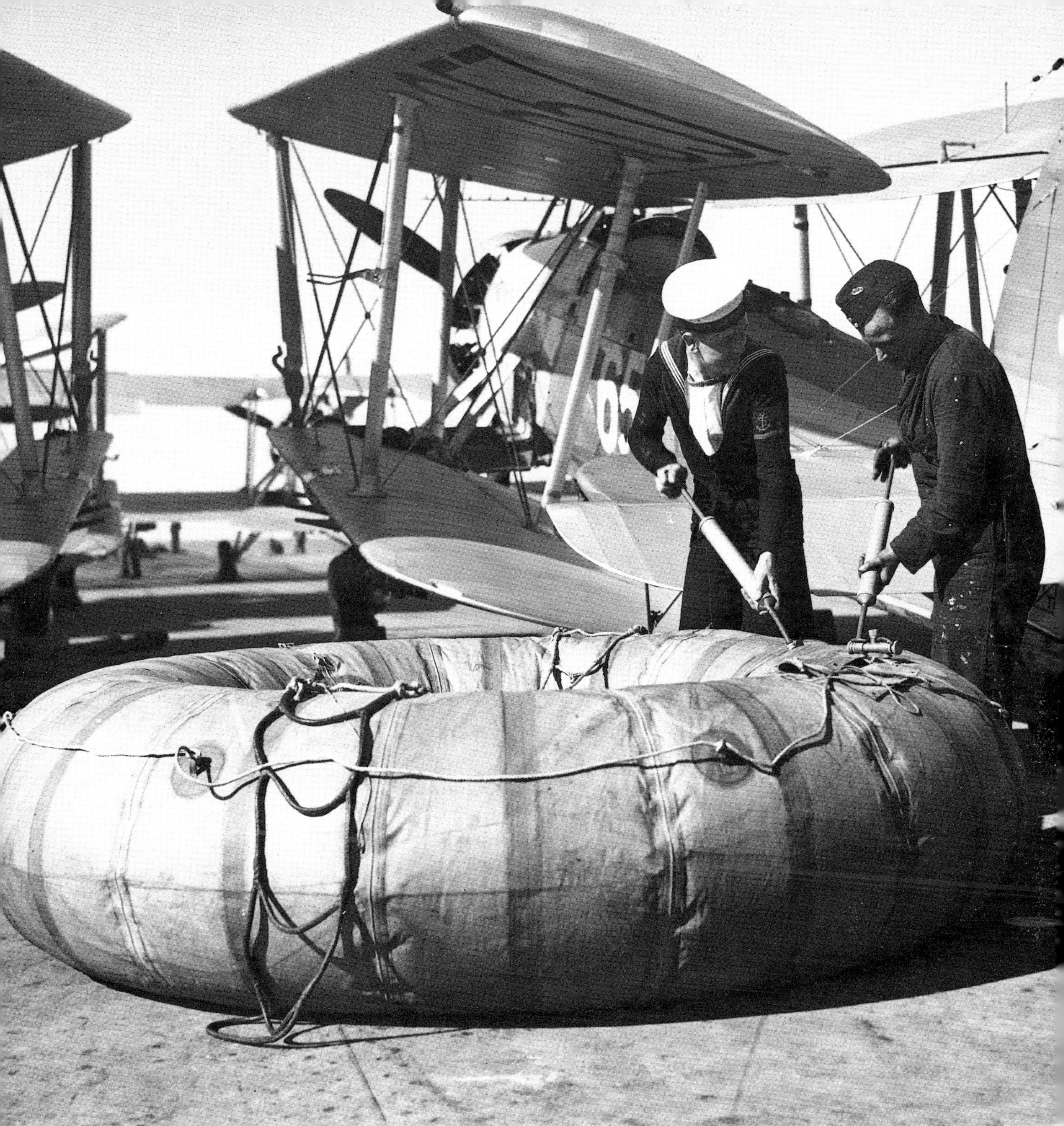

SAFETY EQUIPMENT CHECK
A Fleet Air Arm rating shares the task of checking an inflatable rubber dinghy with an RAF fitter on board an aircraft carrier. Prior to the formation of the Fleet Air Arm the operation of aircraft had been the, albeit shared, responsibility of the RAF.

DE HAVILLAND DH95 FLAMINGO

de Havilland DH95 Flamingo entered airline service in 1939 with Jersey Airways; three were also built for the Air Ministry to be used by the King's Flight and by No. 24 Communications Squadron. The war curtailed further development of the design which had a loaded weight of 17,600 lbs and was capable of 239 mph.

GLOSTER GLADIATOR IIs

Gloster Gladiator IIs of No. 33 Squadron which was re-constituted as a fighter squadron in March 1938. Based at Ismailia it was the only fighter squadron to be operated overseas since 1926. In September a flight was detached to Ramleh in Palestine for ground strafing and patrol duties in response to riots there. The Squadron was in the forefront of the air fighting when war broke out in the Western Desert in June 1940, still flying its Gladiators.

BLACKBURN SKUA IIs
Blackburn Skua IIS of No. 803 Squadron, Fleet Air Arm airborne from *H.M.S. Ark Royal* in 1939. When war broke out the *Ark Royal* sailed for Norway and carried out anti-submarine operations in the North Western Approaches.
Two Skuas were lost on September 14th whilst they attacked the submarine U-30.
The Skua was the first British monoplane designed specifically for dive bombing, it could drop one 500 lb bomb. The type remained in service until 1941.

SUPERMARINE SPITFIRE Is *(opposite)*
In September 1939, No 65 Squadron became operational with Spitfires at Hornchurch. This photograph must have been taken shortly after the Squadron received its new equipment; the Spitfire in the foreground, K9906, was flown by R. R. Stanford Tuck who would later become a celebrated fighter leader.

FZ H
FZ A
FZ P
FZ O
FZ L

HAWKER HURRICANE I

In February 1940 the Blenheim Is of No. 601 Squadron were replaced by Hurricanes; photographed here at Tangmere, No. 601 Squadron would soon find itself in action, firstly when 'A' flight joined No. 3 Squadron in France as the German advance through the Low Countries began and later when the Squadron was in action throughout the first and second phases of the Battle of Britain. After fighting with great distinction the Squadron was retired to Exeter in September 1940.

A vital link in the chain between the drawing office, the workshop and the final delivery is the test pilot whose skill, courage and knowledge makes a success of many marginal projects.
Here P. E. G. Sayer poses in the cockpit of a Hawker Tempest V at Langley.

MARTIN B-26B MARAUDER

Martin B-26B Marauder, 296142 of the No. 397 Bomber Group of the United States 9th Army Air Force flying in support of the Allied advance through the low countries. The black and white stripes, carelessly painted on the wing and fuselage were specifically to identify "friend" in the hectic summer of 1944.

Avro Lancaster B3, ED 592 on a test flight.

MN686

UNSUNG HEROES
A group of relieved RAF Bomb disposal personnel. During the summer of 1940 the RAF formed small flights to deal primarily with unexploded bombs dropped on or near its airfields. Three 500 kilogram bombs suggest that they had had a busy day.

FIGHTER PILOTS
During the summer of 1940 the nation placed great reliance on the efforts of the RAF's fighter pilots in turning the Luftwaffe attacks into defeat. This newsworthy photograph, although posed, does show very clearly and in great detail, the typical attire of the time.

HAWKER TYPHOON IB MN
Hawkei Typhoon IB MN 686 probably on a factory test flight in 1944.

BOULTON PAUL DEFIANT *(opposite)*

The Defiant fighter entered service with the Royal Air Force in July 1939 and it enjoyed the distinction of being the RAF's first fighter equipped with a four-gun turret, introducing a new concept in two-seat fighter in which no forward armament was carried. In action in May 1940, the Defiant enjoyed some success as a day fighter but when German fighters found the types weak spots, losses mounted to a critical level and in August the Defiant became a night fighter.

In this role equipped with A.I. radar, Defiants scored the highest number of kills for interception during the winter of 1940-41. Some thirteen squadrons operated Defiants at night whilst many were used as Air/Sea Rescue and a variety of other duties throughout the war.

HANDLEY PAGE HAMPDEN

Handley Page Hampden was the last of the twin engined monoplane bombers to enter service in the RAF before World War II. The prototype flew in 1936 and by 1940 fourteen squadrons of Bomber Command were operational with the Hampden. The aircraft carried a crew of four and could carry a maximum of 4,000 lbs of bombs some 1,200 miles. The last Hampden raid was in September 1942, but the type continued in use, however, with Coastal Command until December 1943.

GRUMMAN MARTLET Mk I

In December 1940 Lt. L. V. Carver RN and Sub-Lt. Parke RNVR, flying Martlets, succeeded in forcing down a Junkers Ju.88 over Scapa Flow. This was to be the first victory scored by a pilot flying an American fighter in the British Forces and the beginning of a legend, and a successful career, for the Martlet in the Royal Navy. The Martlet, known as the Wildcat in the US Navy, entered service with No. 804 Squadron in September 1940.

PERCIVAL PROCTOR III
Percival Proctor III photographed in a most exhilarating evening skyscape.

LOCKHEED HUDSON Is
Lockheed Hudson Is of No. 6 (Coastal) OTU based at Thornaby in 1941.

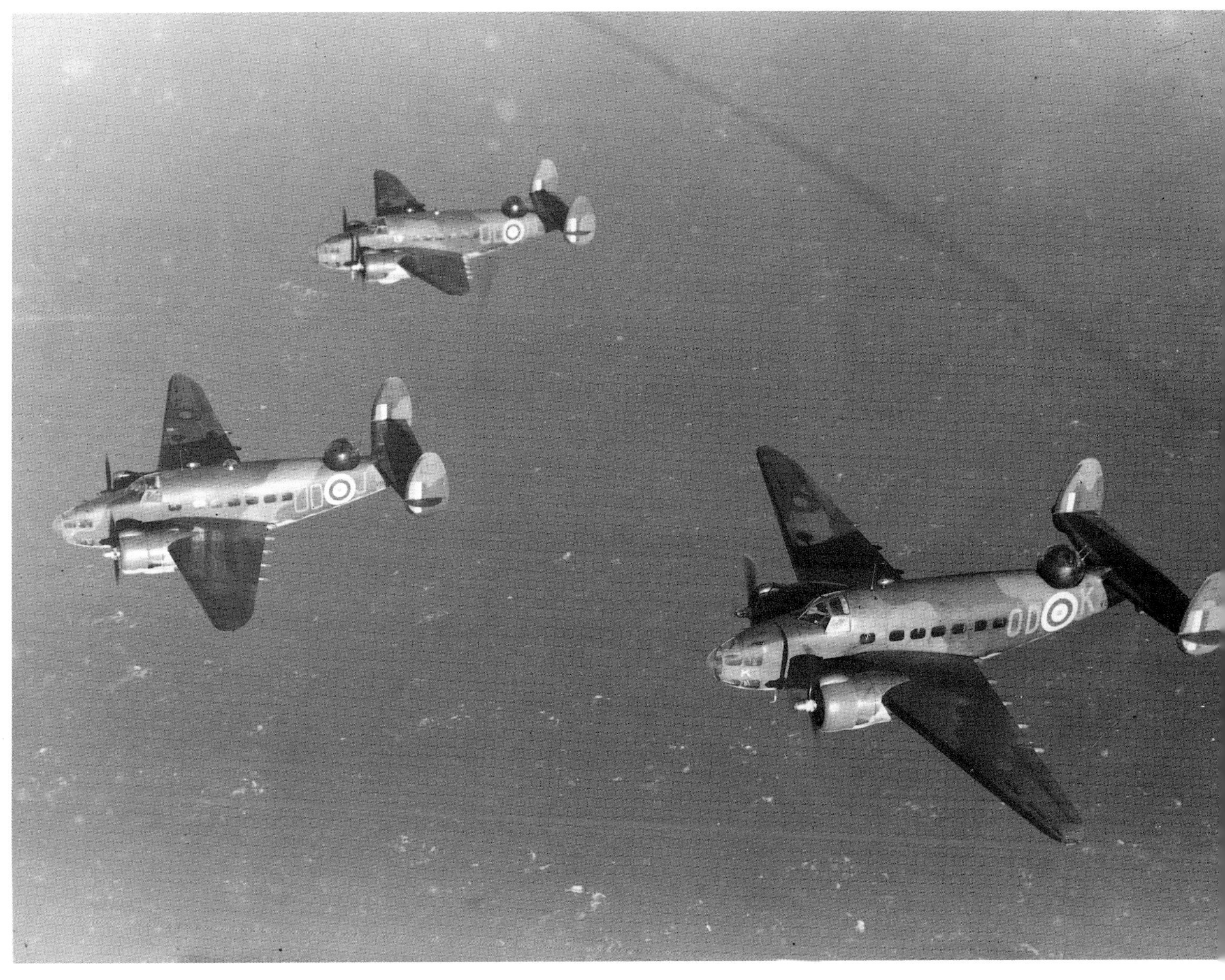

LOCKHEED HUDSON I

Lockheed Hudson Is of No. 6 (Coastal) OTU flying from Thornaby in 1941. The Hudson was the first American aircraft to be used operationally by the RAF during the Second World War and was introduced into Coastal Command squadrons in 1939. Some 350 Hudson Is were followed by larger orders for improved variants. These remarkable aeroplanes not only enjoyed early success with Coastal Command in the U.K., they became widely used in the Middle East, Far East, Ireland, West Africa and the West Indies. After they finally became operationally redundant many were used as transports and for operational training.

SUPERMARINE SPITFIRE V *(opposite)*
Supermarine Spitfire V R6923 poses for Charles Brown's camera over Southern England. The aircraft is from No. 92 Squadron which was based at Biggin Hill in February 1941 when this photograph was taken.

SUPERMARINE SPITFIRE V
No. 92 Squadron, equipped with Supermarine Spitfire V aircraft, form up for this silhouette photograph over Southern England. The Squadron was based at Biggin Hill in February 1941.

SUPERMARINE SPITFIRE V
Supermarine Spitfire V R6923 poses for Charles Brown's camera over Southern England. The aircraft is from No. 92 Squadron which was based at Biggin Hill in February 1941 when this photograph was taken.

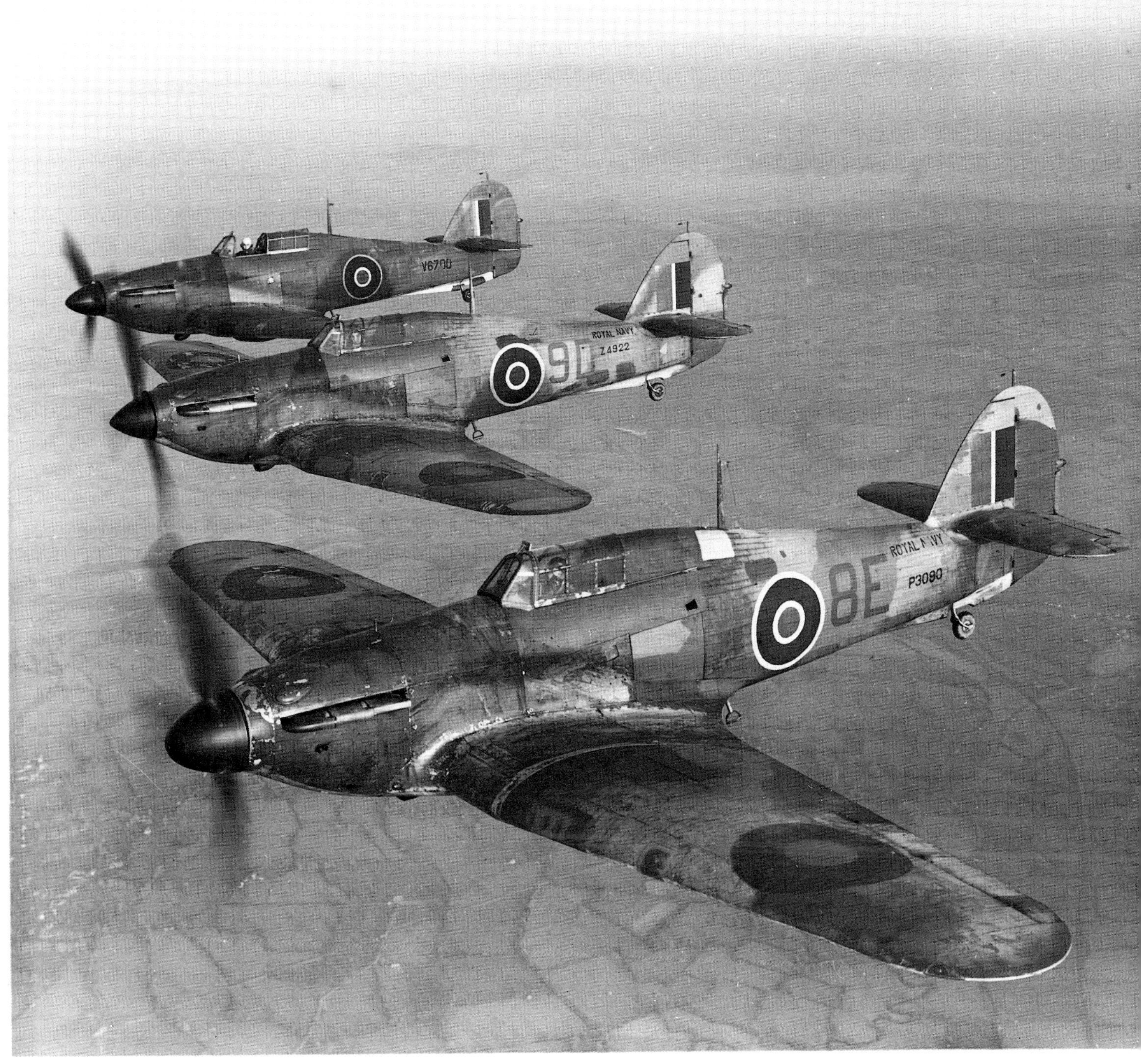

HAWKER SEA HURRICANE IBs

Sea Hurricanes were in many cases Hurricane I's that had already survived the Battle of Britain and were repaired and with the minimum of modification, catapulted from merchant ships or flown from carriers dispersed in convoys for their protection. The losses were high but the presence of Hurricanes successfully reduced the number of bombing attacks convoys were subjected to. These Sea Hurricanes are from No. 760 Squadron, Fleet Air Arm, based at Yeovilton in November 1942.

HANDLEY PAGE HALIFAX BIII
Handley Page Halifax BIII on a test flight from Handley Page's factory airfield at Radlett in April 1944. The Halifax proved to be one of the great bomber aircraft of the Second World War. The prototype first flew in 1939 and the type was put into production in 1940. In all some 29 Squadrons operated Halifaxes, including the MkIII. They were flown by pilots of the Royal Canadian Air Force in No. 6 Group, by No. 8 Group, the Pathfinder Force and equipped squadrons of No. 100 (Bomber Support Group).

SUPERMARINE SPITFIRE VB *(opposite)*
In 1941 deliveries of the Mk V Spitfire began and the type was used intensively in fighter 'sweeps' above the Low Countries in 1941-42. Its speed at low level was increased in its clipped wing form, in which most VBs were to be found in 1943 when this photograph was taken of BL 479 of No. 316 (City of Warsaw) Squadron, then based at Northolt.

X SZ

MITCHELLS IIs

North American Mitchell IIs of No. 180 Squadron lined up on the runway at Foulsham. The first Mitchells went to Nos. 98 and 180 Squadrons at West Raynham in September 1942 and in 1943 they moved to Foulsham. From there they carried out many successful day bombing attacks on suitable targets in France, Belgium and Holland.

VICKERS WARWICK I BV285
A production order for 250 aircraft was placed in 1941 for a replacement for the Wellington bomber: when production began in 1942 the design was well behind the Air Ministry requirements but was of value in Coastal Command. Powered by American-built Double Wasp, engines the first Warwicks were supplied to No. 280 Squadron at Langham in Norfolk in 1943. Some 350 Mk I Warwicks were equipped for Air/Sea Rescue duties.

HAWKER TYPHOON IB

Hawker Typhoon IB became one of the most respected close-support aircraft of the Second World War. Powered by the complex Napier Sabre 24-cylinder 'H' engine capable of 2,000 bhp, the Typhoon could achieve 412 mph. As an interceptor fighter, which it was initially designed to be, it was not a success but with its ability to carry four 20 mm guns plus two 1000 lb bombs or eight 60 lb rocket projectiles it became a lethal weapon when used in support of the Allied advance through France and Holland in 1944. This version has the early cockpit canopy which was later changed for a clear sliding bubble.

DE HAVILLAND MOSQUITO IV DK 338
The MkIV was the first light bomber version to enter squadron service with No. 105 Squadron based at Swanton Morley. This particular photograph was taken in December 1942, a year after the type had entered service.

FAIREY FIREFLY I.
Fairey Firefly I Z2035 photographed in May 1944.

TYPHOON PILOTS
Typhoon Pilots of No. 257 Squadron based at Warmwell pose in front of Typhoon IB JP 682 in August 1943.

PERCIVAL PROCTOR MkIV, LA 589
This aircraft was a prototype of the final version of the Proctor used in RAF service and was photographed in August 1943. The Proctor was a military version of the Vega Gull and was used, from October 1939 as a communications aircraft. Built of wood, the Proctor had a cruising speed of 140 mph, could accommodate four people and was powered by a 210 hp de Havilland Gipsy Queen II engine. In all 256 Proctor IVs were built, the last of which were retired from service in 1955.

MITCHELLS IIs

North American Mitchell IIs of No. 180 Squadron based at Foulsham in July 1943. Some 800 Mitchell light bombers were delivered to the RAF and were used on daylight raids with No. 2 Group of Bomber Command and later as close-support bombers with the 2nd Tactical Air Force during the Allied advance through the low countries in 1944. The first squadrons to receive the Mitchell were Nos 98 and 180 and in all six squadrons received the type which was introduced in September 1942 and superseded by Mosquitos in 1945. Powered by two Wright Cyclone GR-2600 A-5b engines the Mitchell could carry a 6000 lb bomb load 950 miles at around 210 mph.

VICKERS WARWICK I
Vickers Warwick I photographed in B.O.A.C. service in July 1943. The Warwick was designed as a replacement for the Wellington bomber; however, they were not used in that role as there developed within the RAF a growing need for transport aircraft. In 1943, fourteen Warwicks were converted for use by B.O.A.C., who operated the aircraft on mail services to North Africa.

VICKERS WARWICK 5 PN 811

Vickers Warwick 5 PN 811 of No. 179 Squadron was photographed in December 1945 when the squadron was based at St. Eval. No. 179 Squadron was the first to receive the type in November 1944, for anti-submarine work.

SUPERMARINE SEAFIRE IIc's and a HAWKER SEA HURRICANE Ib
Supermarine Seafire IIc's and a Hawker Sea Hurricane Ib flying in formation on 18 November 1942. The aircraft are from No. 760 Squadron, Fleet Air Arm, based at Yeovilton.

SUPERMARINE SPITFIRE MkXII *(opposite)*
The Supermarine Spitfire MkXII was the first operational variant to be fitted with a Rolls-Royce Griffon engine capable of producing 1,735 h.p. at 1,000 feet.
Two Squadrons operated the MkXII and this aeroplane, MB882, was the last MkXII built, it was supplied to No. 41 Squadron. The MkXII was intended for use in counter attacking low-flying Focke-Wulf FW190 sneak-raiders.

PILOTS OF THE FLEET AIR ARM *(opposite)*
Two Seafire pilots confer on the flight deck of *HMS Indomitable* in March 1943.

SUPERMARINE SEAFIRES
Man-handling Seafire IIbs on the flight deck of *HMS Indomitable.*

7H

CHANCE VOUGHT CORSAIR

Chance Vought Corsair of No. 1830 Squadron showing an impressive head-on view of the type. This was the first Fleet Air Arm Squadron to review the type, in June 1943, which was to become a valuable weapon in the Navy's armoury.

SUPERMARINE SEAFIRE IIs *(opposite)*

A splendid photograph of a Seafire flying low over *HMS Indomitable* in March 1943. The *Indomitable* sailed for Gibraltar and the Mediterranean in June 1943 when its fighters flew patrols over the Fleet during the Sicily landings in July. The censor has obviously been busy in deleting details of aircraft and radar.

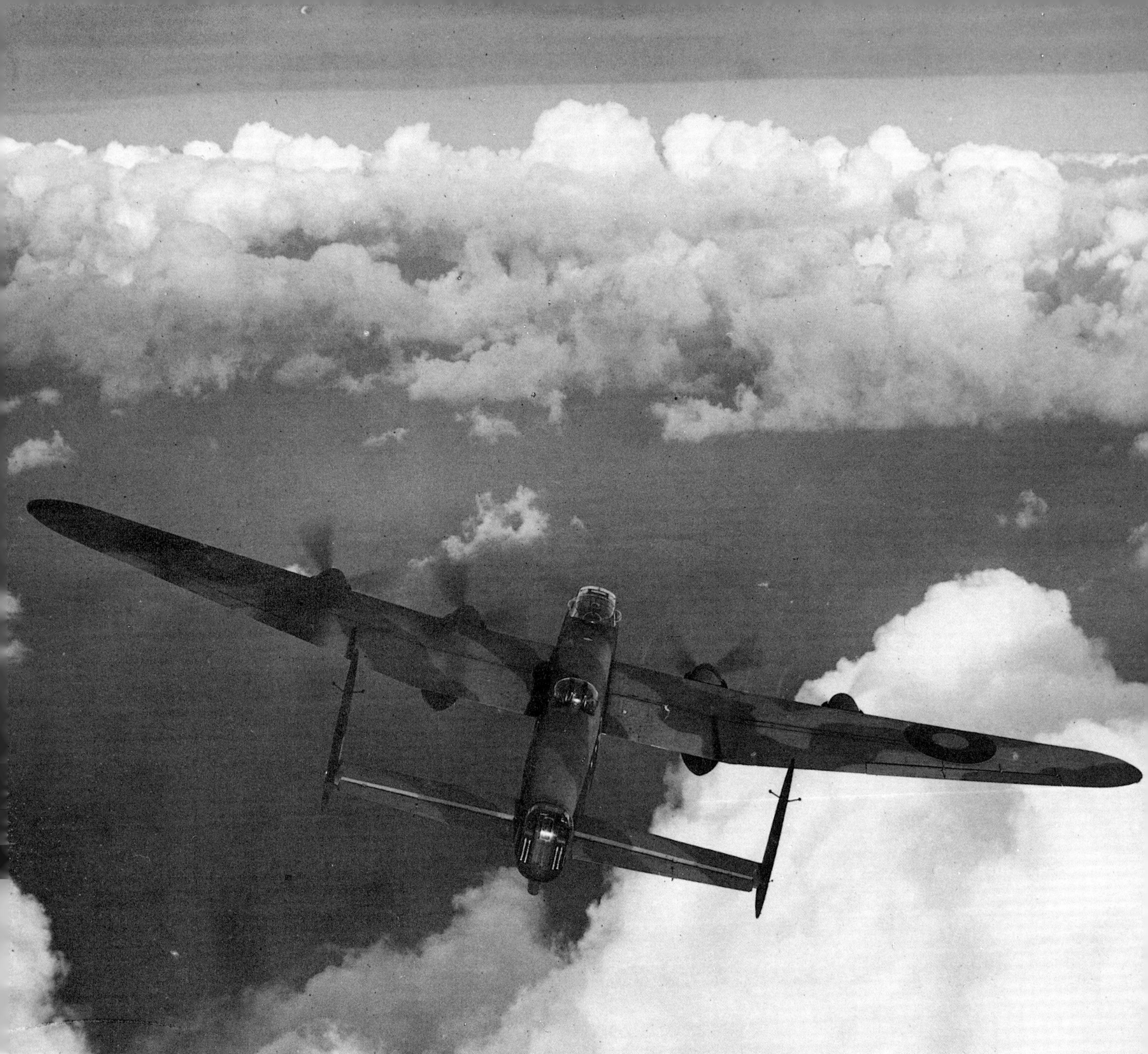

AVRO LANCASTER BIII
Avro Lancaster BIII on a test flight and flying over a superb cloudscape sometime in 1944.

FAIREY BARRACUDA II

Fairey Barracuda II powered by a Rolls-Royce Merlin 32 engine first flew in August 1942 and went into production in 1943. It was the most produced version of the Barracuda and acquitted itself well as a dive bomber for which it had specialised Fairey Youngman flaps which acted as dive brakes when inclined at 30 degrees. The Barracuda had a crew of three, weighed some 11,900 lbs loaded and could carry one 1,620 lb torpedo or four 450 lb depth charges or 6,250 lb of bombs under the wings.

MARTIN B-26B MARAUDERS
Martin B-26B Marauders of the No. 397 Bomber Group on their way to bomb a target in Northern France, August 1944.

DOUGLAS C-53s

Douglas C-53s fly a practice parachute drop. On D-Day, 6th June 1944, and subsequently, the USAAF and the RAF were constantly using Dakotas and their equivalent to drop paratroopers, to tow gliders, to transport personnel, to evacuate wounded and fly spare parts and freight. Developed from the Douglas DC-3 airliner of 1935, the Dakota as the RAF called it, equipped 38 Squadrons and before being largely phased out in the early 1950s, played a major role in the Berlin Airlift.

REPUBLIC P-47 D-30 THUNDERBOLT
The Thunderbolt was widely used both as a long range escort fighter and as a close support aircraft operating ahead of the advancing Allied armies in 1944 and 1945.
The Thunderbolt, powered by a 2,000 hp Pratt & Whitney Double Wasp was capable of 410 mph; it could carry 4000lbs of bombs or 6 rockets and was armed with eight forward-firing .50 inch calibre machine-guns.
In its long range escort role a 200-gallon belly fuel tank was fitted. At 20,000 feet the Thunderbolt was equal to any enemy fighter and superior at altitudes greater than that.

HAWKER TYPHOON IB

Ground crew labour to service a Typhoon of the 2nd Tactical Air Force. All around is the ruin left by the retreating Germans as the Allied advance forced them out of the Low Countries.

NORTHROP P-61A BLACK WIDOW
'Double Trouble', a night-fighter of No. 422 Night Fighter Squadron of the USAAF, cruises over the French coastline shortly after the start of the Combined Allied offensive. This photograph was taken on 28th August 1944.

HANDLEY PAGE HALIFAX *(opposite)*
A Handley Page Halifax photographed from the cockpit of an Airspeed Horsa glider which is on tow. The combination of Halifax and Horsa featured prominently in the Normandy landings of 1944 as well as being used in the invasion of Sicily in July 1943. The glider could carry 20-25 troops and some 3,655 were produced. The final operation involving the type was when 440 gliders landed the 6th Airborne Division across the Rhine in March 1945.

SIKORSKY HOVERFLY I
Sikorsky Hoverfly I was the first helicopter to be used by the RAF. The Hoverfly equipped the Helicopter Training Flight at Andover in 1945. Powered by a 180 hp Warner Scarab engine the Hoverfly could achieve 82 mph.

AUSTER V
During the winter of 1944/45 conditions in the low countries were far from ideal. This photograph vividly shows the ruin in which a unit operating Auster MkVs had to survive.
These aircraft played an indispensable role in artillery spotting and light communication work where their short field capabilities were of considerable value.

HAWKER TEMPEST V

Hawker Tempest V, one of the fastest fighters of the Second World War. The Sabre-powered Tempest V was used from early in 1944 as an effective counter measure against German V1 flying bomb attacks. The Tempest flew with distinction in the Low Countries and 20 Messerschmitt Me 262 jet fighters were destroyed in aerial combat by pilots flying the type. In the photograph is a No. 3 Squadron Tempest in familiar surroundings, its blurred form gives an impression of the relatively high speed this powerful fighter could achieve.

The Squadron was part of 122 Wing 2nd Tactical Air Force which flew over the Low Countries in support of troop advances and on bomber escort work.

VICKERS WELLINGTON IA

Vickers Wellington IA N2857 of the Central Gunnery School to which it was relegated after being superseded in operational flying, now flown as a target for practice fighter attacks. The Wellington IA was similar to the most numerous version of the bomber during the early years of World War II, the Ic.

AVRO ANSON I

The Avro Anson I is well known for its success as an RAF training aircraft during the Second World War, the type was also adopted in 1939 as one of the standard trainers to equip flying schools in Canada. Between 1935, when the first production Anson flew, and May 1952 when the last T.21 was delivered to the RAF, 8,138 Ansons had been built in Great Britain. This scene prominently features an Avro Anson I and was taken at North Weald in 1942.

HAWKER HURRICANE MkV
Hawker Hurricane MkV KZ 193 was one of the eighth production batch produced by Hawker Aircraft Ltd., at Kingston and Langley. The Hurricane MkIV was developed for 'low attack' close support work in North Africa, it could achieve 326 mph, equipped with a tropical filter and two Vickers 'S' guns for use against tanks, thanks to its 1,700 bhp Rolls-Royce Merlin 32.
KZ193 was the second MkIV to be flown and it was subsequently re-designed to make it the first MkV and it was photographed shortly after modification in August 1943.

SUPERMARINE SPITFIRE VB

Supermarine Spitfire VB AD233 of No. 222 Squadron which was based at North Weald when this photograph was taken in March 1942. This particular Spitfire was adopted by Squadron Leader R. M. Milne DFC who commanded the Squadron until May of that year.

SUPERMARINE SPITFIRE VB
Supermarine Spitfire VB of No. 222 Squadron being readied for flight at North Weald during the spring of 1942.

AVRO LANCASTER B1s
Avro Lancaster B1s of No. 207 Squadron which received the type in June 1942 as a replacement for the Avro Manchester with which the squadron was equipped.

HUNTING PERCIVAL JET PROVOST

The Hunting Percival Jet Provost XD674 first flew in June 1954 and was photographed in August of that year shortly before it was demonstrated as the RAF's first jet engined basic trainer at the SBAC Air show at Farnborough.

The first RAF student to solo on a jet aircraft did so in October 1955; since then the Jet Provost has proved an invaluable training aeroplane and is still in use thirty years later.

HANDLEY PAGE VICTOR I

Handley Page Victor I, XA918 was the second of 50 production aircraft and was photographed cruising at altitude in January 1957. The first Victor BIs, entered service with the RAF in November 1957 when they were delivered to No. 232 Operational Conversion Unit at Gaydon and thence to No. 10 Squadron at Cottesmore. In 1965 the introduction of the B2 version of the Victor released the BIs for conversion to in-flight refuelling tankers. Four bomber Squadrons used the Victor BI.

SHORT SHETLAND PROTOTYPE
Short Shetland Prototype, DX166, photographed in May 1945 at a Press demonstration. Despite its huge size and a wing span of 150 feet, the Sheltand was fast and manoeuvrable and the largest British flying boat constructed at that time. This aircraft was used for transport duties whilst the second prototype flew as a luxury passenger-carrying flying boat for a short while.

GLOSTER METEOR MkIV
Gloster Meteor MkIV EE521 photographed in May 1948 shortly after the type entered service with the Royal Air Force.
The Meteor was the RAF's first jet fighter and the MkIV fitted with up-rated Rolls-Royce Derwent 5 engines was to equip 24 Squadrons.

THE FAIREY SPEARFISH
The Fairey Spearfish was a large aeroplane designed as a replacement for the Barracuda. Only three were built as a production order for 140 was cancelled in 1946. The prototype RA356 first flew in July 1945 and Charles Brown's photograph claims to be the first air-to-air of the type (not to be published until February 14th 1946).

SUPERMARINE SEAFANG

Supermarine Seafang, intended as a replacement for the Seafire it was capable of 475 mph at 21,000 feet. Only eight were produced although the Fleet Air Arm ordered 150 in May 1945. The aircraft photographed is the prototype fitted with a Rolls-Royce Griffon 61 engine.

SHORT SUNDERLAND GRV
Short Sunderland GRV of No. 230 Squadron flies majestically over the Aircraft Carrier *H.M.S. Vengeance.*

FAIREY FIREFLY T.1 TRAINER

Fairey Firefly T.1 Trainer was used principally as a deck-landing conversion trainer with the Fleet Air Arm. The T.1 was introduced in September 1947 and was superseded by the improved T.7 version in 1953.

SHORT SUNDERLAND GRV
Short Sunderland GRV of No. 230 Squadron which was based at Pembroke Dock until 1957, photographed over Gibraltar.

AIRSPEED AMBASSADOR
Airspeed Ambassador G-AGUA, powered by two Bristol engines, could carry 40 to 50 passengers at a cruising speed of 260 mph. This ideally suited the expansion plans of British European Airways who, in March 1952, put them into service on the London-Paris flights. Twenty aircraft were ordered and the AS57 Ambassador was re-named in service, *The Elizabethan*.

GLOSTER METEOR MkIII *(opposite)*
Gloster Meteor MkIII EE 397 which was loaned to Flight Refuelling for trials. This photograph was taken from the rear turret of the modified Lancaster bomber G-33-2 and shows the Meteor perfectly positioned for fuel transfer in August 1949.

HAWKER SEA FURY F10s

Hawker Sea Fury F10s of No. 805 Squadron Royal Australian Navy which reformed with Sea Furies in August 1948 at Eglington. In February 1949 the squadron embarked on *H.M.A.S. Sydney* and sailed to Australia.

AVRO LANCASTRIAN TANKERS
Flight Refuelling Limited acquired 4 Lancastrians which were stationed, after modification, at Shannon, Gander, and Goose Bay. This was in response to the Ministry of Aviation instigating a winter North Atlantic freight service evaluation. A Liberator II flew the first regular weekly freight service between Montreal and Heathrow in February 1948.

ABOARD H.M.A.S. SYDNEY
The aircraft is a Fairey Firefly FR(AS)5s of No. 817 Squadron which was formed in April 1950 at St. Merryn as a Royal Australian Navy Squadron specialising in anti-submarine duties.

SUPERMARINE TYPE 535
Supermarine Type 535 in flight over the 'Needles' skirting the western end of the Isle of Wight. This aeroplane was one of the two prototypes used to develop the Supermarine Swift.

DE HAVILLAND VAMPIRE F.3s
De Havilland Vampire F.3s being readied for flight. The prototype F.3 flew in November 1946 and the type was destined to equip 10 RAF Squadrons. These delightful little fighters were capable of 540 mph at 17,500 feet and with their extra fuel tanks filled, could fly 1,390 miles. The F.3 was to be superseded by the F.B.5 version which began to appear in 1949.

WESTLAND DRAGONFLY
A Westland Dragonfly hovers close to the stern of an aircraft carrier ready to pull aircrew from the sea should any misfortune occur. The Dragonfly was developed from the Sikorsky S51 helicopter and became a valued aircraft in the Fleet Air Arm.

DE HAVILLAND DH110. WG240

In 1946 both the Air Ministry and the Admiralty issued a specification for a swept-wing two-seater all-weather fighter and in September 1951, the prototype DH110, WG236 successfully flew; exceeding the speed of sound in a dive on 9th April 1952.

Two more prototypes were constructed before the production Sea Vixen F.A.W. I aircraft emerged to serve with the Fleet Air Arm, being available in November 1958.

The second prototype was WG240 which first flew in July 1952 and was then grounded for modifications, after WG236 broke up at Farnborough during the S.B.A.C. display. It flew again in 1954 but by then the Air Ministry had decided to adopt the Gloster Javelin as its all-weather fighter.

ENGLISH ELECTRIC CANBERRA T.4
English Electric Canberra T.4 WN467 was the prototype for a dual-control trainer variant of the Canberra B2 bomber. This aeroplane made its first flight on 12 June 1952 and was photographed by Charles Brown in September of that year.

HAWKER SEAFURY T.20
Hawker Seafury T.20, UX818 which was photographed in January 1949. The T.20 was a training version of the Sea Fury, already in service with the Fleet Air Arm and had an elongated canopy to accommodate both the pupil and instructor.

HAWKER P1052 *(opposite)*
Hawker P1052, VX279 photographed on 29th June 1949. This charming little aeroplane was one of a series of prototype jet fighters designed by Hawkers.

FAIREY FIREFLY 4s & HAWKER SEA FURY 10s
Fairey Firefly 4s and Hawker Sea Fury 10s of Nos. 816 and 805 Squadrons in formation on 3rd December 1948.

AVRO TUDOR MkN, *STAR LEOPARD*
Avro Tudor MkN, *Star Leopard* of British South American Airways which was photographed in flight on 9 February 1948.

HANDLEY PAGE HASTINGS PROTOTYPE

Handley Page Hastings Prototype TE580 made its first flight from Wittering in May 1946 and was photographed a few weeks later. The Hastings was to succeed the Avro York in RAF Service as the standard long-range transport aircraft.

AVRO LANCASTER Mk2

Avro Lancaster Mk2, LL735 in use as an in-flight test bed for the Beryl jet engine. The aircraft, one of the last survivors of the B2 version of Lancaster was scrapped in 1950.

De HAVILLAND SEA HORNET

De Havilland Sea Hornet 20s of No. 801 Squadron, Fleet Air Arm in formation on 27th November 1947. A private venture developed just too late to participate in the Second World War for which it had been designed. The Hornet was intended for use as long range fighter in the South Pacific, its exceptional performance ensured that it was available for the post-war RAF and with suitable modification, for carrier use for the Fleet Air Arm.

SHORT SEAMEWS
Short Seamews of the Royal Navy in 1957 when the aircraft were operated from Lossiemouth. First flown in 1953, the Seamew was intended as a simple, rugged, anti-submarine aircraft. Only twenty were ordered and only seven were delivered before the 1957 defence cuts caused the Seamew project to be scrapped.

HANDLEY PAGE (READING) MARATHON

Designed by Miles Aircraft Limited in 1944, the Marathon was a twenty-seater airliner powered by four supercharged Gipsy Queen engines with which the aeroplane could maintain a good rate of climb even if two engines failed.

The anticipated orders were not forthcoming and in 1938 Handley Page (Reading) Limited took over the project. A total of forty production aircraft were sold and three prototypes were built. This splendid photograph was taken in January 1950.

SUPERMARINE ATTACKER FB1s

Supermarine Attacker FB1s of No. 800 Squadron, the first jet fighter squadron in the Fleet Air Arm, receiving their aircraft in August 1951.

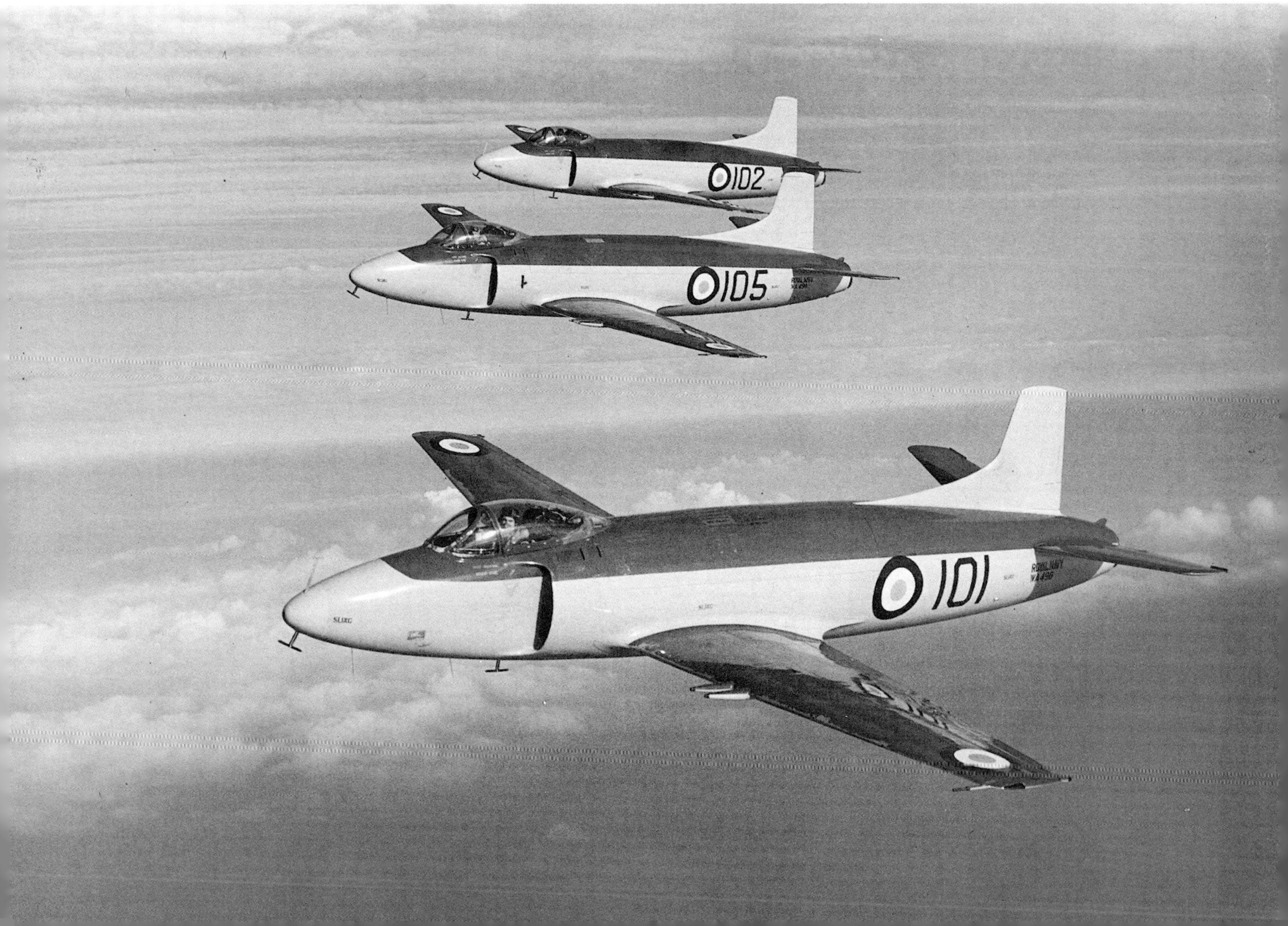

SUPERMARINE SWIFT PROTOTYPE.
Supermarine Swift Prototype WJ960 photographed in August 1951.

SUPERMARINE SWIFT PROTOTYPE WJ960
The Supermarine Swift, Prototype WJ960, was the first British swept-wing fighter to enter service with RAF. Powered by a Rolls-Royce Avon engine the prototype WJ960 first flew in August 1951. The first production Swift F.1 was ready for delivery in August 1952. There were difficulties with the aircraft and only one fighter Squadron No. 56, received the type. By May 1955 the Swift was withdrawn and only the fighter Reconnaissance Mk5 version remained in RAF service.

VICKERS TYPE 757 VISCOUNT

Vickers Type 757 Viscount of Trans-Canada airlines who used their aeroplanes on a triangular service between Eastern and Western Canada and New York, which opened in 1955. Envisaged as long ago as 1944, the Viscount 630 first flew from Wisley in 1948 and the type 700, in February 1949. It was the first gas turbine powered aeroplane to be used for civil transport and was immensely successful entering airline service all over the world.

HUNTING PERCIVAL PRINCE *(opposite)*

The Hunting Percival Prince was developed as a feeder-liner and executive transport aircraft. The Prince first flew in August 1948. Powered by Alvis Leonides engines the Prince could cruise at 155 mph carrying eight passengers and a crew of two. The RAF adapted the design and a modified version called the Pembroke entered service in 1953, forty-four were produced.

VICKERS VANGUARD

Vickers Vanguard G-APEB *Bellerophon* was built to an order placed for 20 Vickers type 951 aircraft in 1956. The order was placed by British European Airways who subsequently changed their requirements for new developments incorporated in the Type 953. The Vanguard first flew in 1959 and went into service with BEA in March 1961 and could carry 126 passengers plus five aircrew, 1,550 miles at 380 mph at 21,000 feet; powered by four Rolls-Royce Tyne engines.

GLOSTER METEOR F Mk4

Gloster Meteor F Mk4 VZ389 practises in-flight refuelling for the 1950 SBAC Airshow held at Farnborough. The fighter was fitted with a nose probe through which fuel was passed under pressure as soon as it made contact with the tanker's drogue.

USAF BOEING YKB-29T TANKER

A USAF Boeing YKB-29T Tanker refuels three Gloster Meteor fighters simultaneously over the United Kingdom. The Meteors were specifically fitted with nose probes for refuelling and various experiments were carried out during 1951.

HAWKER SIDDELEY A.W. 650

Hawker Siddeley A.W. 650 civil transport aircraft, in flight prior to its appearance at the S.B.A.C. show at Farnborough in 1959. Named the Argosy, the type would find favour with the RAF and a number were also operated by BEA on short-haul freighting duties.

HUNTING PERCIVAL PROVOST
The Hunting Percival Provost was designed as the RAF's standard basic trainer and the first prototype WE522 flew in February 1950. The type was superseded by the Jet Provost, the last of 387 aircraft built was retired from RAF service in November 1969.

FAIREY FIREFLY
Fairey Firefly of No. 817 Squadron is prepared for launch on the flight deck of *H.M.A.S. Sydney.*

HAWKER HUNTER F.4

Hawker Hunter F.4 which was the first mark of Hunter to be capable of carrying stores below the wings, including extra fuel, first flew in October 1954. The type entered service with the RAF in 1955.

ENGLISH ELECTRIC PIB

English Electric PIB, of which there were three prototypes, first flew in April 1957 and one, XA847, became the first British aircraft ever to fly at Mach 2.0. The development work carried out with the S.B.5 and the PIA cumulated in the Lightning so named in 1958, the maker's designation being PIB. Powered by two Rolls-Royce Avon engines the aircraft could achieve 1,500 mph at 36,000 feet and could be armed with two 30mm Aden guns plus packs for two de Havilland Firestreak missiles, 48 2-in rockets or two additional Aden guns.

SCOTTISH AVIATION TWIN PIONEER

Scottish Aviation Twin Pioneer first flew on 25 June 1955. This quaint aeroplane was designed as a sixteen passenger civil transport with a range of 398 miles. In RAF service the 'Twin Pin' would find much use both in the U.K. and overseas where its short take-off and landing characteristics were of great value. The Twin Pioneer was finally retired from front-line duties in 1968. A few examples are still flying in commercial hands.

DE HAVILLAND DH108 SWALLOW

De Havilland DH108 Swallow was designed to provide in-flight experience with tailless, swept wing configurations aircraft. The Swallow suffered from compressibility in the trans-sonic speed range and the second aircraft, a high speed version, broke up over the Thames Estuary in September 1946 killing the pilot Geoffrey de Havilland. VW120 was constructed in 1948 and was the third Swallow produced: it set up a new 100-Km closed circuit speed record of 605.23 mph, and in September 1948 became the world's first jet aircraft to exceed Mach I.

BRISTOL BRIGAND I
Bristol Brigand I RH754 was one of the first eleven aircraft built in 1945. The Brigand was initially equipped as a torpedo-bomber but by the time this photograph was taken in September 1947, this aeroplane was about to end its service in that role, with Coastal Command.
When converted into light bombers these fast, heavily armed aircraft were used in squadron service in the Middle and Far East until 1954 when a total of 146 had been built.

SUPERMARINE SPITFIRE N-32 *(opposite)*
Supermarine Spitfire N-32 was one of a small number of MkVIII Spitfires that were converted into two-seat trainers, the instructor occuping the newly-introduced rear cockpit.
The MkVIII was introduced in 1943 and was designed to use the Rolls-Royce Merlin 61 engine which gave this fighter-bomber Spitfire a maximum speed of 408 mph at 25,000 feet. Several variations were developed before a total of 1,658 aircraft were completed. The MkVIII was operational until 1945.
This conversion of the MkVIII was photographed in January 1947 when on trials.

N32

DE HAVILLAND VAMPIRE I

De Havilland Vampire I TG278 was operated by No. 247 Squadron at Odiham when this photograph was taken in August 1945. This particular aircraft was the fourth production aircraft completed; however the design would be produced and developed into nine marks and would equip a total of 36 RAF Squadrons. The type was used widely, in Germany, the Middle East, the Far East as well as by Fighter Command and units of the Royal Auxiliary Air Force. The first production Vampire left the factory in April 1945 and the last, MkIX, in 1953.

BLACKBURN N.A. 39
Blackburn N.A. 39 low level, high speed strike aircraft which was to become known as the Buccaneer in production. The prototype first flew in 1958 and the Fleet Air Arm used the Buccaneer until 1968 when they were operated by the Royal Air Force.
The last three Buccaneers left the factory in 1976 when they were known as the products of Hawker Siddeley and the aeroplanes are still in service.

VICKERS VALIANT
The prototype Valiant WB210 made its first flight in May 1951 after only three years development. This aeroplane was destroyed during a test flight in 1952 and the flight testing continued with the second prototype WB215.
The work carried out on these aircraft enabled the company to construct five pre-production Valiant B.1s in 1953 and by September 1955, No. 138 Squadron was able to take part in a fly-past at the S.B.A.C. show; the first 'V' bomber was in service. This photograph was one of Charles E. Brown's favourites.

VICKERS VALIANT B.2

Vickers Valiant B.2, WJ954 was designed specifically as a low-level pathfinder bomber and made its debut, after a very rapid development period, at the 1954 S.B.A.C show. These photographs of the only B.2 were taken just prior to its appearance.

HANDLEY PAGE VICTOR BI *(opposite)*
Handley Page Victor BI. The first production Victor XA917 made its maiden flight in February 1956. Intended as a long range medium bomber for the RAF the Victor carried a crew of five and could achieve a speed of Mach 0.92. The first B1 entered RAF service with No. 10 Squadron at Cottesmore in April 1958. Bomber Command used the type to equip four squadrons.

VICKERS VALIANT
Vickers Valiant WB215 first flew from Wisley, Vickers factory airfield in April 1952 and was inspired by an Air Ministry order for 25 production aeroplanes, placed in 1951.

BRISTOL TYPE 175 BRITANNIA
Bristol Type 175 Britannia G-ALBO. This giant turbo-prop airliner was photographed in June 1952. Known as the 'whispering giant' the Britannia was first used in its airliner role by British Overseas Airways Corporation in whose colours it is portrayed.

EON TYPE 5 OLYMPIA 4 SAILPLANE *(opposite)*
Eon Type 5 Olympia 4 sailplane was detail developed for the 1956 World Championships. This example is captured on film over Lasham.

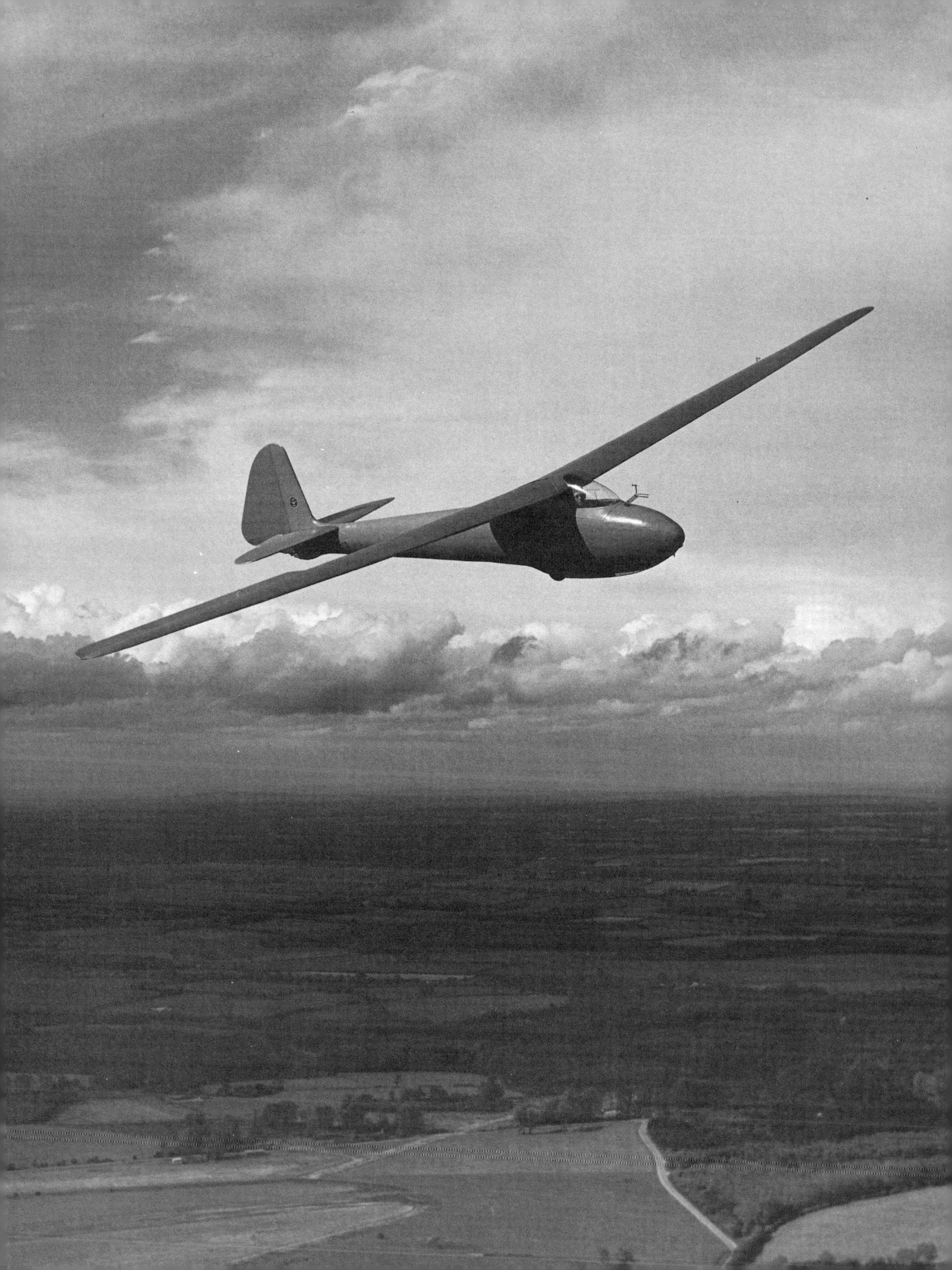

HAWKER SEA HAWKS

Hawker Sea Hawks of No. 800 Squadron, Fleet Air Arm, carrier based on *H.M.S. Ark Royal.* These FGA 6s are caught by the photographer in the process of starting their engines which always sent impressive plumes of smoke from their starters. The squadron operated the Sea Hawks from 1956 to 1959.

AVRO VULCAN B1 *(opposite)*

The prototype Vulcan first flew in August 1952 and was ordered by the RAF as one of its 'V' class aircraft for Bomber Command. This study was one of Charles Brown's favourite photographs and it is not hard to judge why as the white painted Avon-powered prototype VX 770 poses high above Southern England. Some 45 B1 aircraft were completed by April 1959 when the improved B2 became available.

EON TYPE 10 460/463 SAILPLANE
Eon Type 10 460/463 sailplane was designed primarily for the 1965 World Championships.

DE HAVILLAND SEA VENOM
De Havilland Sea Venom was the Royal Navy's first all weather jet fighter. Fifty F.A.W. 20s were built and in service by June 1955 while production switched to the F.A.W. 21 and 22, which by the time construction ceased some 256 aircraft had been completed. The Sea Venom equipped 12 Squadrons of the Fleet Air Arm, being finally retired from Carrier duties in December 1960.

FAIREY FIREFLY FR(AS)5s
Fairey Firefly FR(AS)5s of No. 817 Squadron and Hawker Sea Furies on the flight deck of *H.M.A.S. Sydney.*

EON TYPE 5 OLYMPIA I SAILPLANE

Eon Type 5 Olympia I sailplane being towed over the Hampshire countryside from Lasham in the late 1950s. The Eon Olympia I was originally designed in 1939 by Hans Jacobs and was produced as the Chiltern Olympia DFS 70.

WESTLAND WYVERN S.4.
Ninety production Wyverns were assigned to the Fleet Air Arm, entering service with No. 813 Squadron in May 1953. This Squadron would continue to use the type until March 1958, when it disbanded as the last Wyvern Squadron, again operating from Ford.
This photograph was taken in 1953 shortly after No. 813 Squadron received its aircraft.

BLACKBURN BEVERLEY

Blackburn Beverley was developed from the General Aircraft Limited G.A.L. 60 Universal Transport which first flew in 1950. The major difference between the G.A.L. 60 and the Beverley was the use, in the latter, of the British Centaurus engine which much improved its performance.

The Beverley could carry 45,000 lbs of freight or 70 paratroops at a maximum speed of 238 mph at 5,700 feet. Its great value was in being able to carry heavy or bulky loads using very small airstrips. The RAF favoured the design and ordered 47 which were built between 1955 and 1958. Five Squadrons operated the aeroplane, the last being withdrawn in 1968.

HAWKER SIDDELEY ARGOSY C.Is

Hawker Siddeley Argosy C.Is make an imposing sight when seen from this angle. The Argosy was designed as a main airlift vehicle and a tactical transport and was developed from the Armstrong Whitworth A.W. 650 Civil Transport which was first flown in 1958. In RAF service the Argosy equipped six squadrons and was used from March 1962 until 1974.

The Argosy could carry up to 69 troops or 29,000 lbs of freight at a maximum cruising speed of 268 mph.

FAIREY GANNET
Fairey Gannet was the first aircraft in the Fleet Air Arm to operate in both the search and strike role. The prototype flew in 1949 and in 1951 the type was ordered into large scale production. Four marks of anti-submarine Gannet were introduced into 15 Squadrons of the Fleet Air Arm, the last Squadron to use the type was No. 847 which disbanded in January 1960.

HAWKER SEA HAWK F.1

Hawker Sea Hawk F.1 WF191 of No. 806 Squadron taking off from the flight deck of *H.M.S. Eagle* in February 1954.

HUNTING PERCIVAL JET PROVOST T.1
Hunting Percival Jet Provost T.1 being flown for trials in primary jet training techniques at No. 2 F.T.S. at Hullavington. XD674 was the first aircraft of the initial production batch of ten and was delivered to the RAF in 1955.

ENGLISH ELECTRIC P.1B
English Electric P.1B posing for this beautiful photograph prior to the 1958 S.B.A.C. show at Farnborough. The P1B development, the Lightning, was the first British single-seat fighter to be put into service capable of exceeding the speed of sound in level flight.

HAWKER SEA HAWKS
Hawker Sea Hawks of No. 738 Squadron practising formation aerobatics, in their red painted aircraft, for the 1957 S.B.A.C. Airshow at Farnborough.

SLINGSBY T51 DART
Slingsby T51 Dart, an elegant 15-metre span glider of wooden construction developed for competition work in the early 1960s. This example is flying near Lasham airfield where Charles Brown produced many of his gliding photographs.

ENGLISH ELECTRIC LIGHTNING F.1s
English Electric Lightning F.1s of No. 74 Squadron which had the distinction of being the first Squadron to receive their Mach 2 fighters in June 1960.

ENGLISH ELECTRIC LIGHTNINGS
English Electric Lightnings of No. 74 Squadron, the first squadron to receive these aircraft. The squadron lost no time in painting them in their own distinctive black and yellow markings. June 1960.

HAWKER SIDDELEY P.1127 KESTREL

Hawker Siddeley P.1127 Kestrel was the world's first strike and reconnaissance fighter capable of vertical take-off and landing. Two Prototypes plus four pre-production aircraft and nine production Kestrels were constructed for trials in 1964. The success of these trials encouraged a production order for the now world famous Harrier. This photograph must be one of the last Charles Brown took of a high performance military aircraft in flight.

The Charles E. Brown Photograph Collection

The Royal Air Force Museum was greatly privileged in 1979 when Charles E. Brown agreed to transfer to it the ownership of his magnificent collection of photographs. As the curator with responsibility for the Museum's photographic archives, I must admit to some feeling of excitement at the prospect of receiving such a great hoard of aviation pictures, which, as well as their artistic value, would contain so much information. I and my colleagues were not disappointed, for while many of the photographs had been published a great many more had not, and indeed some of the colour shots dating from World War II had never seen the light of day since their return from the processors. Charles E. Brown was best known as an aviation photographer and will probably always be thought of as such, but the totality of his work shows him to have been much more than that. He was a great all-round photographer who covered many other subjects just as well, ranging from society debutantes of the 1920s through circus scenes, railways, ships and industrial sites. In all of these he had a style of his own, making them readily recognisable as his work.

I was extremely pleased when Tony Harold told me of his plans to produce the first volume of *Camera Above The Clouds* as I was anxious to see these marvellous images made available to a wider public, and at the same time ensure that due homage should be paid to a great photographer. My pleasure was thus doubled when I learned that the book had been so well received that this second volume was to be published. I hope it gives as great a pleasure to all those, aviation fanatics or not, who look at these beautiful pictures.

R. F. BARKER
Keeper of the Royal Air Force Museum

Photograph Reference Numbers

The following is a list of the reference numbers of the photographs reproduced in CAMERA ABOVE THE CLOUDS Volume 2 which are held at the RAF Museum.

All enquiries about obtaining prints of these photographs should be addressed to the RAF Museum and not to the publishers.

The Royal Air Force Museum, Aerodrome Road, Hendon, London.

Page	*Reference*
15	5777-2
16	5620-4
17	5507-4
18	5540-12
19	5620-7
20	5648-11
21	5540-9
22	5761-11
23	5707-8
24	5700-4
25	5873-1
26	5750-8
27	5732-7
28	Not Known
29	5769-2
30	5769-11
31	Not Known
32	5683-17
33	Not Known
34	5651-14
35	5791-17
36	5761-14
37	5804-7
38	5919-4
39	Not Known
40	Not Known
41	5827-19
42	5620-12
43	5827-6
44	Not Known
45	5867-4

Page	*Reference*
46	5839-2
47	5846-3
48	5884-7
49	P100763
50	P100469
51	P100026
52	P100409
53	Not Known
53A	Not Known
54	5908-5
55	5899-2
56	5926-12
57	Not Known
58	5918-7
59	5918-1
60	5903-14
61	5903-11
62	5903-14
63	5946-3
64	5995-7
65	5973-2
66	5972-8
67	5969-4
68	5980-12
69	P100149
70	P100201
71	P100406
72	P100507
73	P100489
74	P100683
75	P100684

Page	*Reference*
76	P100592
77	5984-5
78	Not Known
79	Not Known
80	5990-3
81	Not Known
82	5952-8
83	5977-14
84	6015-12
85	6134-9
86	6021-11
87	299-33
88	6018-1
89	6030-9
90	6040-4
91	300-2
92	6024-9
93	P100695
94	P100016
95	P100363
96	P100601
97	P100599
98	P100023
99	P100113
100	P100357
101	6205-2
102	6100-12
103	6093-4
104	6098-9
105	6388-1
106	6221-1
107	6392-2
108	6228-3
109	6342-9
110	6300-6
111	6325-2
112	6312-7
113	6349-2
114	6263-4
115	6545-4
116	6482-6
117	P100184
118	P100375
119	P100381
120	P100206
121	P100043
122	P100326
123	P100032

Page	*Reference*
124	P100161
125	6628-10
126	6372-12
127	6456-1
127A	6456-7
128	6454-7
129	6454-8
130	6276-4
131	6586-7
132	6814-3
133	6419-3
134	6446-4
135	6810-5
136	6472-9
137	6311-14
138	6626-12
139	6731-2
140	6617-12
141	P100144
142	P100082
143	P100616
144	P100172
145	6785-9
146	6451-5
147	6530-1
148	6538-12
149	6650-4U
150	6606-3
151	6598-2
152	6584-8
153	6777-2
154	6797-1
155	6522-8
156	6313-9
157	6159-5
158	6519-5
159	6625-4
160	6852-11
161	6497-5
162	6543-7
163	6570-14
164	6773-1
165	6729-1
166	Not Known
167	6840-3
168	6840-10
169	6857-4

Index

This Index covers both CAMERA ABOVE THE CLOUDS Volume 1, ISBN 0 906393 31 0 and CAMERA ABOVE THE CLOUDS Volume 2, ISBN 0 906393 50 7.